TRICERATOPS

A Buddy Book
by
Richard M. Gaines

ABDO
Publishing Company

VISIT US AT

www.abdopub.com

Published by ABDO Publishing Company, 4940 Viking Drive, Edina, Minnesota 55435. Copyright © 2001 by Abdo Consulting Group, Inc. International copyrights reserved in all countries. No part of this book may be reproduced in any form without written permission from the publisher.

Printed in the United States.

Edited by: Christy DeVillier
Contributing editors: Mike Goecke, Matt Ray
Graphic Design: Denise Esner, Maria Hosley
Cover Art: Patrick O'Brien, title page
Interior Photos/Illustrations: page 4: Oil painting by Josef Moravec; pages 6, 7 & 19: Joe Tucciarone; page 9: Maria Hosley; page 13: Corbis; page 15: ©Douglas Henderson; page 17: Denise Esner; page 21: ©Douglas Henderson from *Riddle of the Dinosaur* by John Noble Wilford, published by Knopf; page 23: John Sibbick; page 25: ©Douglas Henderson from *Dinosaurs, A Global View* by S&S Czerkas, published by Dragon's World; page 26: Larry League, Dakota Dinosaur Museum Curator, Dickinson, North Dakota.

Library of Congress Cataloging-in-Publication Data

Gaines, Richard, 1942-
    Triceratops/Richard M. Gaines.
       p. cm. – (Dinosaurs)
    Includes index.
    ISBN 1-57765-489-7
     1. Triceratops—Juvenile literature. [1. Triceratops. 2. Dinosaurs.] I. Title.

QE862.O65 G35 2001
567.915'8—dc21

00-069983

TABLE OF CONTENTS

WHAT WERE THEY?

Triceratops
try-SAIR-uh-tops

Triceratops horridus means "horrible three-horned face." This dinosaur had three sharp horns on its huge head. It would use these horns in battle.

The Triceratops could bite very hard. But not as hard as the mighty Tyrannosaurus rex.

The Triceratops was one of the biggest plant-eating dinosaurs. An adult Triceratops weighed about 10,000 pounds (4,536 kg). This big dinosaur stood about 10 feet (3 m) tall. It was about 25 feet (8 m) long.

An adult Triceratops was about the same size as an adult elephant.

The Triceratops's big leg muscles helped it run very fast. This dinosaur could run 30 miles (48 km) per hour. It could walk as fast as a person.

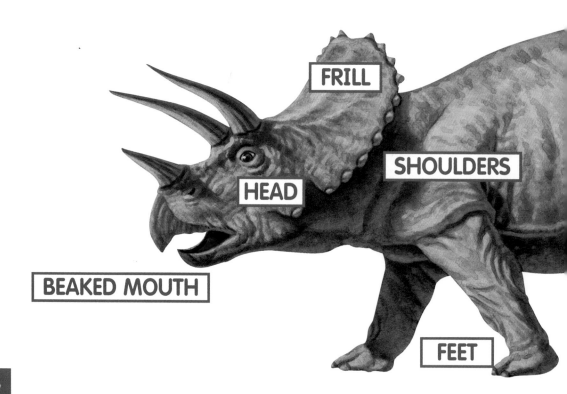

FRILL

SHOULDERS

HEAD

BEAKED MOUTH

FEET

The Triceratops ran on all four legs. Its front legs were shorter than its back legs.

This dinosaur had very wide shoulders. These shoulders were three feet (one m) wide. The Triceratops's shoulders helped it run on legs that were different sizes.

TAIL

LEGS

7

WHY WAS IT SPECIAL?

The Triceratops had a giant head. Its head was 6-10 feet (2-3 m) long. This dinosaur could move its huge head in almost any direction.

The back of the Triceratops's head was like a hard plate. We call this plate a frill. This frill helped to keep the Triceratops's head safe.

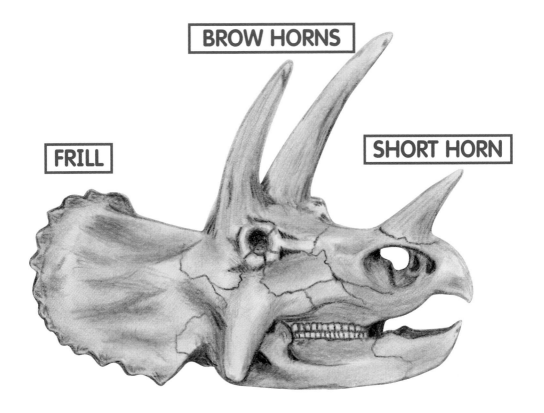

BROW HORNS

FRILL

SHORT HORN

The Triceratops's had three long horns on its head. It had one horn over each eye. We call these brow horns. The other horn was over its nose. We call this horn the short horn. All three horns could grow up to four feet (one m) long.

WHERE DID THEY LIVE?

The Triceratops lived in North America 65 million years ago. That was during the late Cretaceous period.

The Triceratops walked on land that is now the United States and Canada. The Triceratops did not go south of present-day Colorado. It went as far north as present-day Alberta, Canada.

The Triceratops walked around in herds. They stayed close to the lowlands of the Colorado Sea.

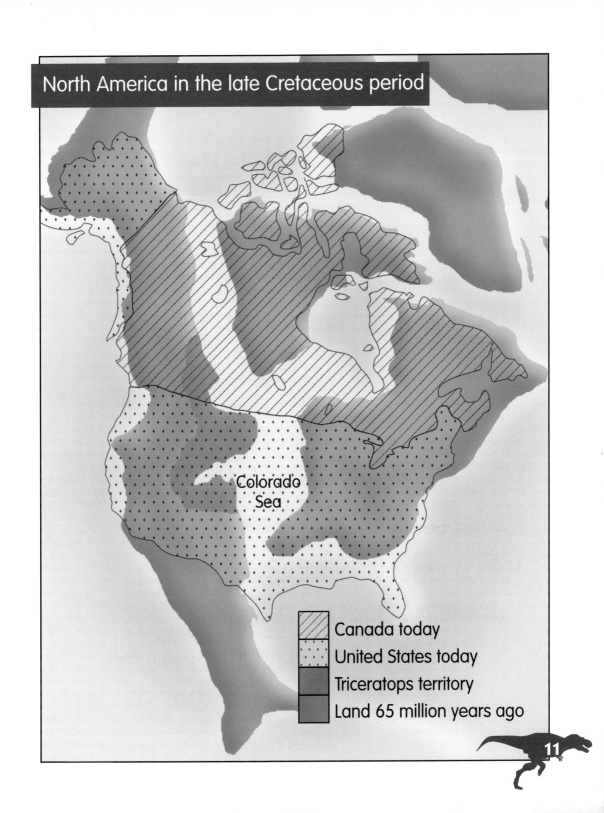

North America in the late Cretaceous period

Colorado
Sea

Canada today
United States today
Triceratops territory
Land 65 million years ago

11

Termites lived with the Triceratops 65 million years ago.

Termites worked together. They formed large groups, or colonies. These termites built mounds that were up to 12 feet (four m) high.

Termites eat dead wood. They like to eat trees. Yet, they cannot eat evergreen, or conifer, trees. So, 65 million years ago, these termites only ate trees like ginkgoes and cycads.

A giant termite mound.

The termites caused many ginkgoes and cycads to die out. Yet, ginkgoes and cycads are still around today.

The termites did not have a lot of enemies. Only the ants hunted the termites.

THEIR DINOSAUR NEIGHBORS

The Maiasaura lived among the Triceratops. The Maiasaura were very large, too. They could grow to be 30 feet (9 m) long. An adult Maiasaura was 6-8 feet (2-3 m) tall and weighed about 5,000 pounds (2,268 kg).

The Maiasaura were duck-billed dinosaurs. This means it had a beak like a bird. The Maiasaura ate plants with this beak. It could store food in its cheeks.

Maiasaura means "good-mother lizard." Indeed, the Maiasaura were good mothers. These dinosaurs took care of their eggs until they hatched. Fossil hunters have found bones of Maiasaura near its young, eggs, and nest.

Maiasaura caring for their young.

WHO ELSE LIVED THERE?

The Coniophis is a snake that lived in the time of the Triceratops. It is the earliest snake we know about. This early snake is related to the pipesnakes of today.

The Coniophis was a short snake. It had a thick head and a stubby tail. This early snake had a few sharp teeth.

Many people believe snakes used to be more like lizards. Maybe these early lizard-like animals lived underground.

Over many years, perhaps these animals lost body parts that got in the way. For example, maybe they did not need legs, ears, and eyelids when they lived underground. Is this how they changed into snakes? Nobody is sure.

pipesnake

17

WHAT DID THEY EAT?

The Triceratops ate ferns, vines, and young trees.

The Triceratops walked around in herds eating plants, or grazing. They ate plants, vines, and young trees that grew close to the ground. A few of these plants were ferns, cattails, and palmettos.

This plant-eater ate with a beak. The Triceratops's beak was covered with horn matter. This beak was good for plucking or grabbing plants.

Then, the Triceratops could | BEAK | store these plants in its mouth. This dinosaur would chew the stored food with its special mouth. This mouth could cut up the food like scissors.

The Triceratops had strong teeth. They could eat tree trunks and woody branches with these teeth.

The leading enemies of the Triceratops were the Tyrannosaurs. The Tyrannosaurs were bigger than the Triceratops. The Triceratops had to watch out for Tyrannosaur dinosaurs like the Tyrannosaurus rex.

The Triceratops used its horns to fight enemies. Yet, it probably could not win a battle with the Tyrannosaurus rex.

Tyrannosaurus rex hunts a Triceratops.

The Triceratops belonged to a family of dinosaurs. We call this family the Ceratopsians.

One Ceratopsian dinosaur was the Torosaurus. The Torosaurus's head was nine feet (three m) long. This dinosaur did not have three horns like the Triceratops. The Torosaurus had only one horn over its nose. It had one other horn over its eyes.

Another cousin of the Triceratops is the Pentaceratops. It had the same three horns as the Triceratops. Yet, the Pentaceratops had two more horns. These horns stuck out from each side of the Pentaceratops head.

The Pentaceratops was a very large dinosaur, too. It weighed about 10,000 pounds (4,536 kg).

23

Many of the horned dinosaurs lived in Mongolia and China. Millions of years ago, Mongolia's climate was warm and dry like a desert. These dinosaurs moved to North America to escape the desert.

The Psittacosaurus lived in Mongolia and China about 95 million years ago. This plant-eating dinosaur was about four feet (one m) tall. It walked on two legs. It also had a narrow, horny beak.

24

The Protoceratops lived in Mongolia millions of years after the Psittacosaurus. The Protoceratops was seven feet (two m) tall. It weighed about 1,000 pounds (454 kg). This dinosaur walked on all four legs. It had a beak like the Triceratops and the Psittacosaurus.

Psittacosaurus

Fossil of a Triceratops head.

Othniel Marsh was a famous dinosaur fossil hunter. In 1887, someone brought some fossils to him. The fossils looked like two horns. Othniel Marsh thought these horns belonged to an old giant buffalo.

Later, Othniel Marsh received a second fossil. This fossil was a complete head with three horns. Othniel Marsh figured out that these fossils matched the first horn fossils.

Othniel Marsh discovered that all of these fossils did not belong to a buffalo. Instead, they belonged to a dinosaur. In 1889, he named this new horned dinosaur Triceratops horridus.

Not long after, people found many more Triceratops fossils in Wyoming, Montana, South Dakota, and Colorado. People found Triceratops fossils in Canada, too.

Museum of the Rockies
Montana State University
600 W. Kagy Blvd.
Bozeman, MT 59717
www.museumoftherockies.org

Dickinson's Dakota Dinosaur Museum
200 Museum Drive
Dickinson, ND 58601
www.dakotadino.com

**Cretaceous Hall of the American
Museum of Natural History**
Central Park West at 79th Street
New York, NY 10024
www.amnh.org

Canadian Museum of Nature
Victoria Memorial Museum Building
240 McLeod Street (at Metcalfe Street)
Ottawa, Ontario, Canada
www.nature.ca

TRICERATOPS

NAME MEANS	Horrible Three-horned Face
DIET	Plants
WEIGHT	10,000 pounds (4,536 kg)
HEIGHT	10 feet (3 m)
TIME	Late Cretaceous Period
FAMILY	Ceratopsian
SPECIAL FEATURE	Huge head with horns
FOSSILS FOUND	USA—Colorado, Montana, South Dakota, Wyoming Canada—Alberta, Saskatchewan

Triceratops lived 65 million years ago

First humans appeared 1.6 million years ago

Triassic Period	Jurassic Period	Cretaceous Period	Tertiary Period
245 Million years ago	208 Million years ago	144 Million years ago	65 Million years ago
Mesozoic Era			Cenozoic Era

Zoom Dinosaurs
www.EnchantedLearning.com/subjects/dinosaurs
Zoom Dinosaurs, designed for students of all ages, includes an illustrated dinosaur dictionary and classroom activities.

Thunder Lizards: From Science to Fiction
www.thunderlizards.com
Information on Triceratops and other dinosaur-related facts are here.

Dinosaur Data Files
www.nhm.ac.uk/education/online/dinosaur_data_fil es.html
These dinosaur data files were designed to be printed out and photocopied for educational use in the classroom or at home.

climate the weather (rain, temperature, and wind) of a place.

conifer trees that have needles instead of leaves. Conifers stay green all year long.

Cretaceous period period of time that happened 144-65 million years ago.

cycads palmlike plants or trees.

dinosaur reptiles that lived on the land 248-65 million years ago.

fossil remains of very old animals and plants. People commonly find fossils in the ground.

fossil hunters people who hunt for fossils.

frill hard plate on beak on back of triceratops' head.

ginkgoes trees with fan-shaped leaves and yellow seeds.

lowlands low or level land.

palmettos fan-leaved palm trees.

INDEX

DATE DUE
